NOT ON YOUR OWN
The Power Of Learning Together

Mary Glover ◇ Linda Sheppard

SCHOLASTIC

Toronto • Sydney • New York • London • Auckland

To Ralph, of course

Scholastic-TAB Publications Ltd.
123 Newkirk Road, Richmond Hill, Ontario, Canada L4C 3G5

Scholastic Inc.
730 Broadway, New York, NY 10003, USA

Ashton Scholastic Limited
Private Bag 1, Penrose, Auckland 6, New Zealand

Ashton Scholastic Pty Limited
PO Box 579, Gosford, NSW, 2250, Australia

Scholastic Publications Ltd.
Holly Walk, Leamington Spa, Warwickshire CV32 4LS, England

Cover illustration by James Hill, design by Terence Kanhai

6 5 4 3 2 1   Printed in USA   0 1 2 3 4 5/9

Canadian Cataloguing in Publication Data

Sheppard, Linda.
　Not on your own: the power of learning together

(New Directions)
1st ed.
ISBN 0-590-73459-8

1. Interaction analysis in education. 2. Elementary school teaching. 3. Classroom environment. I. Glover, Mary. II. Title. III. Series: New Directions (Richmond Hill, Ont.).

LB1027.S48 1990   371.1'02   C90-093818-8

Contents

The classroom as community

Five-year-old Chad labors over a non-fiction piece on cardinals. He's a beginning writer and finds the composition process arduous. Jenny, his volunteer peer writing partner, liberally assists him with letters and sounds. At the end of the writing workshop Chad has written: KRLS R RD (Cardinals are red). The teacher notices his proud expression and exclaims, "That's great!" Chad replies, "Yes, I did it all by myself" — gesturing grandly at his partner — ". . . with a little help from Jenny here!"

At the grand old age of five, Chad and Jenny have a clear understanding of what it means to be a member of a classroom community. They know from experience that learning is a social activity and that learners need others to succeed in their work. The everyday life of their classroom has taught them that pooling knowledge helps them accomplish much more than they do when they work on their own. Chad and Jenny share an outlook on learning and community classroom life that encourages, supports and honors the efforts of every member. They love being an integral part of their classroom community. Without everyone's contribution, their community would have less vitality. They deeply understand that community is the lifeblood of daily classroom living.

Several key elements help to create and sustain a classroom community. These exist simultaneously and are interrelated — prerequisites for and by-products of community.

Collaboration

Collaboration is both a process and a relationship whereby children like Chad and Jenny learn to work together as writers, learners, citizens and human beings. It begins the very first week of school as the children work together to form rules, agree on housekeeping procedures and plan activities; it continues as they work on common projects throughout the year:

- A group of children building a Hopi-style pueblo in the block center find they must plan together, pool their subject knowledge and collaborate on design decisions.

1

- Hours of rehearsal to prepare a play or dance for an appreciative audience bring together several children with diverse attitudes and feelings.

- Mia and Jessie learn the true meaning of collaboration as they help each other make dolls. They transform their egocentric needs into helpfulness as they assist each other with cutting, gluing and holding pieces of cloth in place. While completely intent on their own project, they nevertheless demonstrate cooperative behavior. Their friends see that it's easier to get along than to argue.

Collaboration becomes a way of life as common interests find opportunities for carrying out common classroom business. Interest and opportunity must coexist in a classroom that's a community of learners. As group members work together and share their strengths and weaknesses, they begin to consciously appreciate those they spend their days with at school. They become a community.

A sense of belonging

For children to commit themselves to learning, they need to feel that they belong. Experiencing that the others in the classroom community care about them allows children to see their school environment as a safe place to take risks. Children who are secure members of a learning community know that their teacher and peers will support them — even when they make mistakes or don't know. Community thrives in a classroom where learners are risk-takers and children know they're valued and respected as human beings. They needn't fear rejection or ridicule; they know that if they fall along the way, someone will be there to help. When young children know they're trusted as learners, they strive to reach their potential, knowing that their efforts will be met with interest, acceptance and encouragement.

Classroom life

Young readers and writers thrive in a community that's rich in genuine and purposeful language. The literate behaviors that children engage in during daily classroom life make for community. Literacy means using print to satisfy curiosity and think critically — that is, to live as a learner. It energizes and informs the community as a whole, at the same time encouraging and empowering individual learners to risk and grow.

The everyday business of the classroom places literacy demands on the community in a number of ways:

- Attendance must be taken: "Would our helper read the names of those absent?" . . . "Does anybody know why Sean's not here today?"

- Correspondence from parents needs to be read and acted upon: "Boys and girls, Belinda's mom says we may keep this heart model for two weeks."

- Messages are sent to other staff members: "Mrs. De Angelis, would you please return the book you borrowed as soon as possible?"

- Fresh artifacts and specimens must be acknowledged and dealt with: "After you tell us your horse femur story, would you mind making a collection label for it?"

- Notices get posted: "Emily, would you please make a sign for the money basket for our festival?"

- Letters from penpals and class friends are read: "We received a letter from Ian in Ecuador. Let me read it to you. It looks as if he's written some of it in English and some in Spanish."

- Thank-you letters get written: "We need to write letters to the people who helped us with our Japan study. You can sign up on the chart to write a letter to one of them."

- Class books are signed in and out: "Before you go home make sure you've signed out a book to read for your homework tonight."

Throughout the school day, a classroom community talks and listens, reads and writes. Through dialogue learners wonder, explore, reflect and critique. They work together to construct meaning in ways they wouldn't as individual learners. They read and write notes to one another to convey important messages:

This is Jacob's tumbleweed. Save. It is delicate. It is thorny too.

DONTRE⊗C9T

Don't wreck it.

Dear Linda

Last night [they] didn't have my size cowgirl boot. I have the hat, a bandana, jeans, belt [and] an Arkansas shirt.

To Linda from Megan

They write memos to the school maintenance staff to make requests for repairs, or alert others to problematic situations:

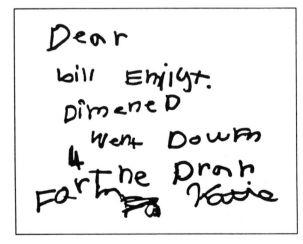

Dear Bill

Emily T's diamond went down the drain.

From Katie

4

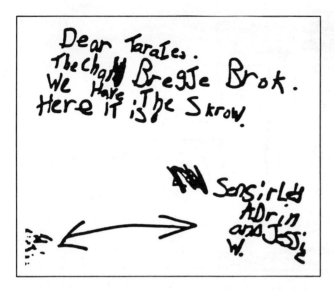

Dear Terry.

The chain bridge broke.
We have the screw.
Here it is.

Sincerely,
Adrin and Jessie W.

They write letters of thanks to express social niceties to class friends and helpers:

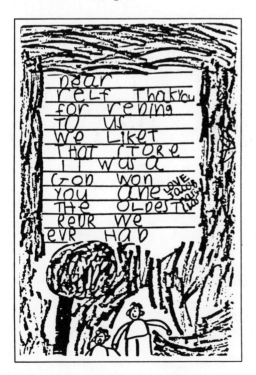

Dear Ralph

Thank you for reading to us. We liked that story. It was a good one. You are the oldest reader we ever had.

Love, Jacob

Janice

I like your helping me.

They make labels for projects and collections to help build community awareness of them:

Afternoon Class's garden

Haunted House

Members of a classroom community understand that their individual and group attention is needed for their own learning to flourish. The business of daily life, and its literate behaviors, keep the community a living, breathing organism.

Shared history

Community grows in proportion to the evolution of a shared history. Courses of study, special events, daily triumphs and tragedies, everyday stories shared, and discoveries made along the way all contribute to the shared history of a class:

- The class is happy for Tara as she proudly displays her two baby teeth the dentist has just pulled. They appreciate her excitement, knowing how desperately she's wanted to add her picture to the tooth graph all year.

- Children talk excitedly, remembering the day Emily's butterfly hatched from the cocoon, or the day they all took turns watching the firefighters extinguish a chemical fire blazing in the building across the street.

Sharing a common body of knowledge about school and the world creates a bond among the members of a classroom community. The shared history secures commitment to other learners and provides the foundation for writing together.

Development of a shared history needs talk. Children and teachers in a classroom community require time and opportunity to tell their stories and hear the responses of other community members. Writing conferences, exchanging ideas during work on a common project, and group dialogue after reading a favorite story are but a few of the situations where talk helps build history and keep the community energized and alive.

Examination/reflection

As with any community, a classroom community lives both an examined and a spontaneous life. We (teachers and children) carefully plan and reflect, then capitalize on frequent surprises. For a study of winter, the children begin to assemble a collection of books that feature some aspect of wintertime. Some begin to notice that all the Russian folk tales on the library shelves belong in the winter book collection. Illustrations show characters in hats, mittens, boots and woolly coats.

Landscapes are often heavily wooded or covered with snow; buildings are thick and substantial, with smoke drifting from their chimneys. As a group, we come to a quick understanding: it's cold in Russia. We want to know more about this chilly place that's contributed so many books to our set of wintertime volumes. Our knowledge and understanding of the folk tales expands as we read about the people and settings that produced them, our own community growing stronger as we learn about the communities of others. More importantly, we come closer to the sense of ourselves as members of a global community, drawn to others by the knowledge we have of them.

Celebration

Community is strengthened, and a wide range of experiences shared, through celebration of individual and group achievements:

- Good books help celebrate special days like Christmas and Halloween.

- Lost teeth are commemorated with explanatory stories of their extraction that are then read to the entire class.

- Approaching birthdays are circled on the monthly calendar in anticipation of their arrival and celebration.

- Individual writing projects, often solitary endeavors in the past, flower when writers read to each other.

- All the children are proud of their group accomplishments. A trilogy of stories on color ("Prisms," "Rainbows," "Primary Colors"), by three groups of writers, becomes a valued addition to each child's home book collection when reprinted for all members of the class.

- The tattered pages of a published collection of poems about Martin Luther King, Jr., reveal the children's delight in that group work.

Through acknowledgement of these accomplishments, the group gains an appreciation of what everyone *can* do. The children are inspired to improve their craft as readers and writers because their efforts have been celebrated by an appreciative audience — *their* classroom community.

Living with literature

When children are actively engaged in learning about topics that interest them, they naturally motivate themselves and others to learn more. They work hard to keep the community going, and put forth their best efforts to maintain a harmonious, caring environment. Over time, meaningful involvement with literature, writing and the content areas (social studies, science, math) are the major elements of this process of community building. In this chapter, we'll focus on the literature component; in the next two, on the writing and content areas.

Sharing

Readers and writers live in a community of shared stories. From what we've seen in our classrooms, we conclude that a group functions as a community when its members are steeped both in the stories of the living, breathing people in it, and in the equally real stories of literature. So we strive to surround ourselves with our own stories and the stories of others, through our own writing and the writing of other people. In this way our own stories are intermingled with those of great authors, and book characters virtually become members of the classroom community.

Even at this young age, a shared history is built through literature, and a reservoir of common experiences with book characters and their adventures accumulates quickly in the classroom. As the world of children's literature opens up, *Frog and Toad* — or those unlikely friends, *Amos and Boris* — quickly become reference points in dialogue about other characters or life events. Children begin to accept these characters as part of their daily lives, and they use them to help extend meaning in other work they do. For example, during a discussion of *Peach Boy*, a Japanese folk tale, Brian comments that it's just like in *Bony-Legs* because, " . . . little Sasha gave the dog bread and Momotaro gave the dog a dumpling."

As the year progresses, we collectively draw from this shared knowledge of story. More books simply add to the shared history and provide an ever larger foundation from which insights are drawn for all new learning by members of the classroom community.

Thinking and feeling

Of all the possible factors, we feel that literature has had the largest impact on us in transforming the chemistry of our classrooms and altering our perspectives about teaching. As we've jointly sought to understand our experiences with literature, we've broadened our response to story to include the *feeling* level as well as the *intellectual*. In response to Gerald McDermott's story of tragically misplaced loyalty in *The Magic Tree*, Khalise breaks the silence at the book's end by whispering, "I feel like I can't breathe."

In our classrooms, children and teachers struggle to discover the meaning of a story, and our collaborative work brings us together. After a kindergarten brainstorming session in which we list the countless themes in *Charlotte's Web*, five-year-old Sarah, seated in front of the chart and amazed at the length of the list, exclaims for all of us, "This is a *great* book we're studying!" Even though the formal reading of the book is over, Sarah uses the present tense. She sees *Charlotte's Web* as a book the class will always study and consider.

As some children share their thoughts about a story, others listen with appreciation. During a dialogue about symbolism in *The Big Wave*, seven-year-old Charlie leaves his classmates (and teachers) speechless as he comments: "Jiya was the *soul* of his family. He was the one who kept his family alive." Charlie's insight into the story enables his classmates to see the value and depth of his thoughts, thus enriching their own understanding of the book.

Understanding the world

The way we use a story has changed from quickly reading it once a day to using it as the heart of the entire curriculum. By using literature to learn about the world, we become members of a greater community of scholars and learn to appreciate the rights and responsibilities of knowledge:

*   A study of aging and the elderly begins with *Wilfrid Gordon McDonald Partridge*, the story of a boy who lives next door to a nursing home. It's enriched and extended through other wonderful books about elderly people and their relationships. The subject of death in old age becomes more understandable to young children through books like *Nana Upstairs, Nana Downstairs* or *Tales of a Gambling Grandma*.

- Multicultural studies are initiated, and children begin to explore the values of other cultures through reading folk tales of different lands. After hearing the Russian folk tale *The Snow Child*, Samuel responds to the setting's exotic quality by commenting to his kindergarten classmates, "I feel like I've been on vacation." During a study of winter, also using Russian folk tales, the children learn about survival under the most difficult weather conditions. Together they see that people are often isolated and lonely, needing to work to overcome the challenges of winter living. They realize that kindness is valued and good-hearted people usually come out ahead in the end. They come to know that people everywhere share the same basic needs and values, regardless of cultural background.

- Through the study of literature, children experience worlds they normally wouldn't know, and travel all over the world without ever leaving the classroom. *Bringing the Rain to Kapiti Plain* offers a poetic glimpse of life on an African plain. Through its beautiful text and illustrations, the children gain access to a way of life much different from their own. Stories like *The Ox-Cart Man* help children to see how, in another time and place, it took hard work to help keep a family provided with the necessities of life. By entering other worlds and other times, our knowledge and sense of the present world is enriched and we're reminded how we fit into the greater world community of the past, present and future.

- Literature helps children see the universals in life. Through books such as *Tight Times* and *A Chair for My Mother*, children recognize patterns in other people's lives similar to those in their own. Through stories shared in our classrooms we come to know that we all have happy times and sad times, experience days when we are worried or days when we feel silly. Literature enables us to experience the entire spectrum of human existence; it tells us that we're not alone. Knowing that we all need each other and have to work interdependently to keep our lives going in a positive direction reminds us that we're all a part of the human community.

Community of readers and writers

By living with and in literature we've come to appreciate our membership in a larger community of writers and readers. Good literature provides an excellent model for writing and talking. The wonderful worlds William Steig creates through his unique use of the English language fill children's heads with amazement. His work inspires children to play with words and try them out, in both their conversation and their writing. Six-year-old Valerie tells her friend to hurry up: "You're *dawdling*," she says, "just like Pearl in *The Amazing Bone*." At age four, Amanda uses the new term "scat" from *Rich Cat, Poor Cat* to describe the movements of Kitty White in *Push Kitty*: "Look, he's scatting!"

Good literature demonstrates to children the best use of language by those who've mastered the crafting of words. Maurice Sendak's *Chicken Soup With Rice* is one of the most familiar books in kindergarten by virtue of its constant use. When asked to write about a party she's been to, Megan authors this poem:

Gary's Birthday

2 cakes in the bowl
with chicken soup and rice.

By Megan Loden

Literature exposes children to different genres, demonstrating the many possible ways we can express ourselves through writing. After reading such delightful books as *Animalia* or *Ashanti to Zulu*, children are inspired to write their own ABC books about winter, aging or the desert. Poetry comes alive for them as they see the three bears and Goldilocks in a whole new light with Jane Yolen's *Three Bears Rhyme*

Book. The Jolly Postman and "The Letter" from *Frog and Toad Are Friends* provide amusing introductions to letter writing. Children are eager to begin writing their own mysteries after reading Thatcher Hurd's *Mystery on the Docks*. And books such as *Good Dog, Carl* or *Ben's Dream* show them that stories can be told without words. They learn that they needn't be limited by their writing abilities, that they can tell stories with pictures. Favorite authors become teachers to all of us in our classroom community.

Literature gives children permission to dream and to build their own imaginary worlds. Chris Van Allsburg, for example, takes us places that our wildest imaginations couldn't have created. In his book *Jumanji*, an innocent-looking game found in the park surprises two children by bringing snakes, rhinos and an erupting volcano (among other things) into their home while their parents are away. *Polar Express*, his Christmas book, paints the essence of our most private dreams about the North Pole and the magic of the Christmas season. Authors such as Van Allsburg, and Maurice Sendak in *Outside Over There*, help us to see that fantasy and imagination offer ways to travel both individually and together. Through entertaining these playful ideas we strengthen our learning community as we learn to tolerate and appreciate the dreams of others.

Metaphor for living

Finally, literature serves as a metaphor for living. The symbols we find in literature help us to understand why the world is the way it is. As we examine and reflect on the stories we share, and those we experience alone, we're able to see options for living our own lives; books offer an overview of the choices. They provide models for responding to the world and show us different ways of coping with the demands of life, bringing the spectrum of human living to our classrooms. Literature, when lived together, celebrates humanity.

ing for knowledge

The afternoon class is reading over a list of Chris Van Allsburg books they've recently studied. The teacher points out the last title they read. One of the children exclaims, "No, that wasn't the last one! The last one we read was The Stranger!" The teacher quickly revises the list and they continue their study for the day by reading another Van Allsburg book, Ben's Dream.

In the previous chapter we examined the role that literature plays in building community; here we'll take a closer look at the daily writing that goes on in our classrooms, paying close attention to the ways writing brings us together as learners.

Writers who know they belong to a community understand they'll be writing for a variety of audiences, depending on the type of writing they're doing. They learn very early that the teacher is only one of many people their writing is intended for, and that it will be different depending on the audience. Our children write to each other, to us, to famous authors, to their families and to others they may not know. They soon discover how to adapt their writing to meet the requirements of different audiences, both within the classroom community and beyond it. A personal note about a problem, written to one of us, looks very different from a poem intended for publication. A thank you letter to a friend who has visited the classroom has a more polished look than a journal entry written between student and teacher.

In our classrooms we see and undertake two very broad categories of writing: group-generated (charts) and individual. We, the teachers, do most of the actual scribing in group-generated writing, with the class determining the content of what we physically record on large pieces of chart paper.

Group-generated writing

Chart writing shows the teacher as both literate model and learning peer in the classroom community. It demonstrates a way of thinking clearly, being thoughtful, and preserving knowledge; it models a way to know and learn. Through the teacher's daily regard for writing as a necessary and valuable pastime, children also come to value writing as a means for communicating and becoming literate.

Language experience charts have been used for a number of years in classrooms around the world. Much of our current work with charts has been an outgrowth of this earlier group-writing routine. However, our daily work with children has led us to be more honest in our teaching and, as a result, our use of charts has changed. We've shifted from creating "chart stories" that had minimal connection to our current classroom studies to giving children control of the chart content. We've moved away from controlling what's on the charts, refocusing our attention away from simply learning language to using language to learn. Our charts no longer seem contrived as we truly begin to hear and record the ideas of children.

We've actually begun to construct a living curriculum on charts. They continue to serve as records of the shared history of our classroom community, ongoing records of daily classroom work, but they've also become valuable reference documents and a forum for restructuring meaning. (The class list of Chris Van Allsburg books mentioned at the beginning of this chapter shows the use of charts for all three purposes.) Furthermore, our charts have become tools for immediate instruction that arises spontaneously out of the current courses of study, allowing us to examine our work over time and reflect on the learning that has taken place.

The charts our classes generate fall into a variety of categories:

Graphs

While graphs are more often used in mathematics or science, we've discovered that they're equally useful in other content areas. They serve as long- and short-term recording devices for classroom activities and patterns: who has had the measles, when baby teeth fall out, how tall the children are.

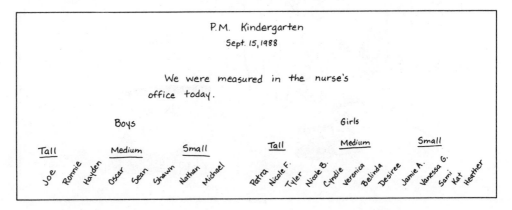

Graphs can record topical inquiries such as "What kind of costume did you wear on Halloween?" or "What are you doing for Christmas?"

Chart graphs also reveal categories.

Your Skeleton		
Supports	Moves	Protects
spine clavicle feet pelvis legs — fibala, femur, patella, tibia	legs — fibala, femur, patella, tibia spine ribs scapula humerus elbow radius / ulna wrist hands feet pelvis	skull ribs sternum pelvis spine

Lists

Lists are much more than itemized information. Characteristics of folk tales, types of songs or poems, book lists (by author, genre, subject, etc.) are good examples:

Cat Books

Push Kitty
Rich Cat, Poor Cat
Mrs. Cat Hides Something
Zoom at Sea
Rotten Ralph
Cross Country Cat
Have You Seen My Cat?
Millions of Cats

Other lists serve as guides for planning daily assignments, preparing class projects and organizing rehearsals for dance or dramatic activities. Lists of rules, when developed by the children, function as a dynamic reminder of group goals for the classroom community. Lists of topics, usage guides for specific writing forms (personal letters, for instance) and lists of frequently used words all serve as valuable reference documents:

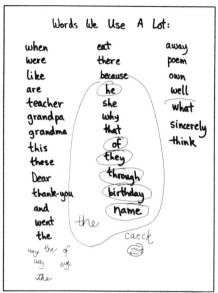

Words We Use A Lot:

when	eat	away
were	there	poem
like	because	own
are	he	well
teacher	she	what
grandpa	why	sincerely
grandma	that	think
this	of	
these	they	
Dear	through	
thank-you	birthday	
and	name	
went	the	
the	caeck	

wey the of
way eye
the

Finally, lists allow examination of a specific subject, as well as reflection on divergent possibilities. Listing the children's answers to the question "What is this book about?" after reading *The Country Bunny and the Little Gold Shoes* helped the children see the range of themes in a book that was superficially about Easter. They were able to respond critically to the value of the book after participating in the listing process:

The Country Bunny and
the Little Gold Shoes
is about:

Easter	dancing + singing
love	cooperation
babies	accidents
the country	trying
gold shoes	working
magic	having lots of kids
places	beautiful
working	stuff
rabbits	being fast
kindness	
traveling	
helping	

Webbing charts

    Webs can be used by a group both to plan studies and to organize or summarize information. They consist of a main topic placed in the center of the page, with radiating lines connecting related informational groups, and can be used either at the beginning or the end of content studies. Their use facilitates the brainstorming process by allowing thoughts and ideas to be made visible, and encourages expansion and development of idea groups. Webbing charts can also serve as research notes for children to organize material for small group writing of reports:

Ireland Research

Summaries

    Summaries are usually written as stories. The forms these stories might take include descriptions of special activities, daily news, upcoming events, retellings of read-aloud stories, and pre- and post-content study knowledge:

June 3

Breakfast in the Park

    We ate in a
shady place under a
tree. We put
blankets. out. We
cleaned up the trash.
    We ate very well.
Yummy, delicious
breakfast !

Teaching diagrams

Teaching diagrams are pictures drawn on charts with the help of input from the class. These drawings, often part of a content lesson, may be consulted again as the study progresses and may be added to as more information accumulates:

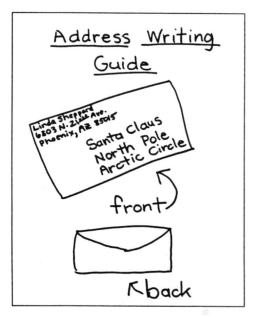

Often a chart can be used for instructional purposes even when its primary purpose is something else: a letter, a class poem, thank-you notes, invitations, announcements, a news article. Mini-lessons are short pre-planned lessons that arise from previous interactions with the class. For example, when students initially learn to do research they need instruction on how to find information. A mini-lesson helps to clarify the process for them.

How to Get Information

- look it up in a book:
  - dictionary
  - encyclopedia
  - magazine
  - books of what you're studying
  - storybooks/folk-tales
  - fiction
- interview someone
- write a letter

- take a trip
- watch a movie
- look at artifacts
- visit a museum
- look at pictures or postcards

Individual writing

Noah has just completed his first piece of fiction, "The Planet Tookie." He shares his writing with his first grade class and it's well received. Later he reflects in his journal:

Dear Mary,

I finished The Planet Tookie yesterday. I was happy. I read it to my mom and she liked it and my sisters liked it too. And my grandma liked it too. I was happy when I finished the pictures for The Planet Tookie. I like when I was writing The Planet Tookie. The Planet Tookie is the most favorite book I wrote. I'm thinking about writing Return to the Planet Tookie next year.

Love,
Noah

Our students observe us writing in the classroom for ourselves and for others. Each day they see us take notes on things they say, send written messages to other staff members, write in our journals at the same time they do, document who has returned their literature study books — all the writing that keeps a classroom functioning properly on a daily basis. They come to see that by being actively engaged in writing we help to maintain our classroom community.

We realize that writers of any age need to have something to write about, someone to help them do it, and someone to hear and appreciate it. Along with our children, we've come to believe that our ideas are valued, that we all have something worthwhile to say. We've grown to understand the value of other people's ideas, and the extent to which we can learn from their writing. We know the joy of what it means to be a writer and the joy of sharing our stories with others. Writing works in our classrooms because we're a community.

In addition to group-generated writing, children conduct their own writing processes in our classrooms. They write for a variety of purposes. Children like Noah learn to understand the responsibility all beginning writers have to themselves and to their audience; they know the value of their work and appreciate readers who share their accomplishments; they realize that writing can record and inform, and that sharing what has been written can be exciting and pleasurable.

Logs

Classroom writers keep a variety of logs that serve as a record of their individual learning history. Logs may be documentary, observational or reflective. Young gardeners, filled with the wonder of sprouting seeds, record the growth of their new plants in a log:

What I saw happening in my jar and in the big jar. This is one of the beans that came out. My bean hasn't come out.

What is happening to the Indian corn. There is 14 Indian corns and some are an inch long. The ones in the big jar are growing like weeds.

Literature logs allow children an opportunity to record personal insights and questions to share later with fellow readers. Five-year-old Megan writes a note about a Russian folk tale, *The Mitten,* to share with her group:

The Mitten

I like this book's cold.

Journals

Journal keeping is one way our children come to know reading and writing. Personal journals epitomize the daily-ness of literacy and help children understand the importance of ordinary events in their lives at home. The old problem of having "nothing to write about" disappears when children write about their own lives. The dialogue that forms between student and teacher through journal entries is illuminating and gratifying. An honest interest in the events and thoughts of another's life builds a lasting trust between learners, providing the all-important sense of belonging.

Mary, it is fun having you for a teacher. Are you proud to be a teacher?

I just thought I would ask. I like you.

I'm interested in dogs, especially when I'm going to have one of my own.

Classroom publications

Experienced with a large body of literature and confident as risk-takers, beginning writers work hard at their craft as they eagerly take on writing for class publication. In a workshop setting they receive instruction, undertake research, conference with their peers and their teacher, and draft stories. Publications may emerge in a variety of genres including poetry, personal narrative, non-fiction, fantasy or documentary. These publications add to the richness of the classroom community.

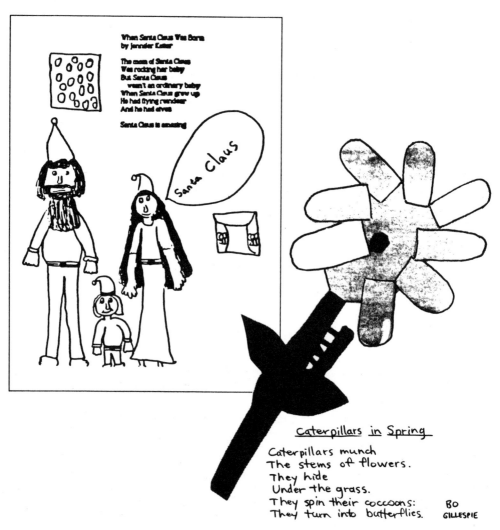

Caterpillars in Spring

Caterpillars munch
The stems of flowers.
They hide
Under the grass.
They spin their coccoons:
They turn into butterflies.   BO GILLESPIE

MY TrIP

bY

JANette CorraL

I went to Bagdad. When I went to Bagdad, we went in a motor home. It took a long time.

Me and my Aunt Sandy got sea sick. Then we were hungry.

We opened stockings in Bagdad. Grandma Evans and Grandma Wood and Grandma Altman and Grandpa Altman--they opened stockings. They have all blue lights.

I had fun at Christmas. I got a Barbie case and Fuzzle Wuzzles. Tommy let me color with his markers.

We came back to Phoenix.

25

The Japan Study
by Mia Segura

Our class is studying Japan. It was one of the kids' ideas to study Japan. We were lucky we had Mica and Jessica Rodd. Then we made books about Japan. We read a book that had Japanese people in it. Its title is The Big Wave.

Young authors grow to understand both the private empowerment and the community-building aspect of writing. All along the way they read their written work to others and listen to the written work of their classmates. We as teachers work alongside them, writing and sharing our own work. In groups we talk about our writing, as peers and partners. The personal becomes enhanced by being public. After reading the lead to his draft of "The Planet Tookie," Noah is inspired by the enthusiastic classroom audience to finish his first piece of fiction.

Recognizing that information must often come from beyond the school environment, individuals write outside the classroom for class studies. Indeed, many of our best group studies have begun with the pooled knowledge children collect as homework from parents, friends and their own book collections.

A study of Martin Luther King, Jr., for example, began in both our classrooms with family memories of the civil rights leader, recorded by our students. Jacob and Noah, sitting on the floor with their teacher and classmates, share the information they've gathered from their previous night's homework assignment, helping their class make a list of what they've found out. After ten or eleven items are listed, Noah asks, "Did Martin Luther King die in his dream?" Jacob turns to him and replies, "No, Noah, he died *because* of his dream." The data they've collected through writing has sharpened their awareness of larger worldly issues.

Even at a very early age, children learn the power of interview as they apply their writing skills to gathering information. They come to know the value of being a writer as they work to bring knowledge of the world into the classroom.

Name ADRIN GREEN

Find out two or three things about Martin
Luther King, Jr.

he Route For SiviL rit's
1.2. he came From a Poor Famaly
3. he LiveD In the South
2. he BeLVeD in Peace

Collaborative writing

Our children sometimes write together in small groups. They may, for example, sign up to write a joint letter to a former classmate or friend, or they may practice their collaborative skills by working in teams to write an article for the school newspaper:

Going to Mary's House
By Jessie Wenz and Jessica Spencer

The first grade class walked to Mary's house. When we got there there was a bunny sitting on the ground. We ate outside. We each got to pick our own orange off her tree. We had lots of fun at her house. The phone rang. Emily answered it. It was Deb from school. Some kids tried to pet the bunny's tail. It ran across the street. Then we had to go back to school.

Two children may share a common interest in a subject and decide to team up for writing purposes. Jessie and Denise express their love for Yvonne, the school "tooth fairy," by publishing a joint book about their experiences with her:

The Tooth Fairy pulls out people's teeth from Awakening Seed. The Tooth Fairy pulled out Jessica S.'s tooth and Jessie's and Charlie's. **YVONNE** is the Tooth Fairy.

She puts the teeth in baggies. She writes your name on the baggies. The Tooth Fairy puts the date on the baggies.

The Tooth Fairy is a teacher at Awakening Seed School. She teaches the third and fourth grades. She and I are good friends.

We trust her. She has the feeling with her finger.

Class books

Children are also involved in individual writing for class books. Often, during content or literature study, a book will be compiled by the group to bring the study to a close and/or summarize each child's impressions of the work. For example, after reading *The Big Wave* the children, their minds full of the language and imagery of the story, wrote poems and painted watercolors depicting their memories of the book. Writing used in this way helps young learners to celebrate their knowledge. When preserved in a class book, it serves as a reminder of the wonderful learning experienced together as a community and becomes a documentation of the shared history of the group.

The Big Wave
by Ben Hackbarth

The Big Wave was thrashing through the mountain.
Jiya went to the mountain.
His family died.
Jiya fell unconscious.
He was asleep for a long time.

The Crashing Waves
by Caitlin Fraser-Reckard

They crash against
the great mountain
that stands against the great wave
the fishermen who lived on the beach
died

The Terrifying Wave
by Noah Underwood

the wave is big
it is tall
it tears down houses
people run
from the Big Wave

Bones
by Brian Evans

when the Big Wave left
there were bones
from the people

some different people
came back

The case for content

The class has just completed a planning web for its study of the human body. Jessie comments, "This web is a lot bigger than the one we made for our Japan study!" The teacher probes for explanation by asking, "Why do you think this happened?" A classmate suggests, "It's because there's more stuff in the body than there is in Japan." Noah immediately replies, "No, it's because we know more about the body than we did about Japan."

The dialogue among these children demonstrates a level of thinking, and a commitment to learning, that you find in classroom communities where meaningful content is at the core of the curriculum. As a group of learners work together to build a common body of knowledge, individuals flourish along with the community. Each person realizes that his/her contribution to the group is important, holding equal weight with that of others. The way a study is undertaken allows freedom for individual choice — each learner is able to pursue personal interests and become an expert in some aspect of the study. As a classroom community's history is built through shared knowledge, each member becomes both a teacher and a learner.

The knowledge that grows inside a classroom community doesn't remain within the walls of that community, but spills out into the world, becoming accessible to parents and families as well. A child's enthusiasm prompts parents to join in the study by sharing their valuable knowledge and experiences. Parents come to realize that they, too, can be teachers and learners and that they play an important role in their child's education. The classroom community expands to include "ex-officio" members.

Classroom content and life outside the school naturally connect, and we must organize our teaching with the idea in mind that the world is our textbook. When we learn from the real world, our awareness grows. Seeds sprout in plastic cups on the classroom window ledge, and suddenly children notice sprouts along their own driveways. The teacher brings in a bouquet of sweet peas and someone exclaims, "My grandma has sweet peas too!" The class learns the body parts of garden insects and now the strange creature under the playground slide is recognized for what it is — a praying mantis on the hunt for dinner. School life and life outside the classroom connect, each informing and enriching the other. Our eyes and minds open to the world as they never have before. Knowing things makes sense. We start to see knowledge as an integrated whole rather then isolated pieces. New information illuminates what exists around us but often goes unnoticed or unconsidered. We realize how fascinating and varied the world is, and the curriculum comes alive.

When real-life pursuits are valued as curriculum possibilities, the classroom becomes a forum, a resource center, a laboratory, a place to reflect, a sanctuary for learners. Content studies allow time for slowing down, examining the world and attending to details. Embedded in the process is a method for inquiry — children learn to ask questions, seek answers from a variety of resources and reflect on daily accumulations of facts and observations. For example, as monthly weather graphs accumulate, they reveal springtime shifts in wind patterns. Noticing this change leads the teacher and children to question why. The next step for the class is to identify a source of local weather information that will shed light on this newly discovered phenomenon. This approach sets the stage for the children to be researchers for life — access to a multitude of resources helps them know and understand the variety of avenues available for exploration.

In content studies, all the elements of literacy come into play. The power and pleasure of knowing and using information leads the curious learner to read, write, talk and listen. No matter how extensive the study we organize, our children want to go further. No matter how sophisticated a concept we imagine we're exploring, our children are capable of understanding even more.

There are many ways to select content studies. As teachers we consider specific topics from a broad range of real-life phenomena. We pay attention to the world around us, keeping our eyes and minds open for possible opportunities. We then make curriculum choices based on years of school experience, selecting issues that are meaningful to us or that we believe children need to know about.

Other factors enter into the picture. Holidays and special events need attention. Children share objects of interest that generate dialogue and questions for further inquiry. Items brought from trips, parents' business journeys or family vacations can be the seed for whole class studies. Stories that children tell of their daily lives also provide excellent starting points for content work. The "Hong Kong" shirt Jenni wears to school, a gift from her grandmother, suggests an inquiry into the different lands where Chinese people live. Picture books with intriguing illustrations and story lines also initiate thought for studies. The specific focus of most studies evolves from the children's ideas. By keeping our minds aware of the range of possibilities, we find an organic, living curriculum at our fingertips.

Some studies are short and primarily focused around seasonal events such as Easter or Grandparents' Day. Others begin as short-term interests and develop into long-term obsessions. A skeletal study, initiated at Halloween, still has significance in April when a newly found coyote skull is brought to class. The children examine the skull before adding it to the science corner's permanent bone collection. The huge canine teeth provoke a brief discussion of previous knowledge of carnivorous animals.

Some concepts are so natural and pervasive that they continue to surface in various forms throughout an entire school year. For example, the broad study of cycles might involve the exploration of human body cycles such as blood circulation or breathing, life cycles of plants and animals, or inquiry into the solar system. In mathematics, children explore the concept of pattern, discovering the cycles that repeat themselves with cubes, small objects or pattern blocks. Cycles also become obvious in literature as we explore books such as Donald Hall's *The Ox-Cart Man*, Tony Johnson's *Yonder* or Mordecai Gerstein's *Mountains of Tibet*.

Stages

Several stages occur in the process of conducting a content study. Sometimes they happen informally or not at all; sometimes they become an integral part of the study. Generally there are five stages: planning, gathering of resources, investigation, expression and celebration.

Planning

The first stage is spent organizing thoughts, ideas and questions. Sometimes we do this preliminary work on our own, but more often than not this part of the study is done with the entire class. If the children are included at this stage, they can make choices about the direction of the experience and see how information can be organized and ordered. For some studies it's helpful to begin by listing what we already know, and what we want to know, about the topic. We've found webbing highly successful in helping young learners get started. Children worked in small groups to create the following planning web for their study of Japan:

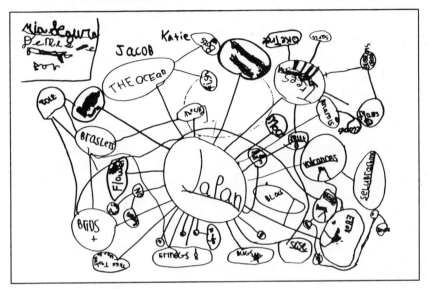

Gathering

Once the focus is determined, it's necessary to collect resources and information. During the gathering stage, we assemble a book collection for our new study. Many books on spring are familiar to children from previous author, genre, seasonal, fine arts or science studies. When a planned spring study narrows to an examination of gardens, all but two of the books are already familiar to the children. The best (and least perishable!) of specimens and artifacts from previous studies, retained in the classroom's permanent collection, appear in a new light. Last fall's spider webs that were found in a flower bed and the seedpods from winter trees are added to the spring table.

An explanation of the spring study goes home as homework, with a request for parental assistance in gathering information and related materials. This process of gathering resources and sharing them with the class gives children an opportunity to make a personal contribution, thus strengthening the whole community as well as the individual's bond to it.

Investigating

As the materials are gathered, the children learn to become researchers, to ask questions and discover where to find the answers. Often, with very young children, the investigating process occurs as a whole class. We take a walk to find signs of spring, first around the school and then around the neighborhood. We look around us and ask "What's happening? What are we seeing right before us?" Flowers are blooming all over the neighborhood and in outlying desert areas. We list all the different kinds of flowers we see in the neighbors' yards; we look at books, we read and write about spring; we try our hands at a flower garden of our own.

The books go on the "Spring Garden" table along with vases of flowers brought from home, butterfly cocoons, feathers, dried bees' and birds' nests. We cut pictures from current newspaper stories on spring wildflowers in the desert; we collect other photographs from magazines and calendars. As our study of spring progresses, it changes its emphasis from plants and flowers to birds and insects that seem to be always present when we examine photographs of gardens, read stories about them and visit real ones. While investigating spring flora, we begin to learn more about birds and insects. Upon close examination, our flowers yield seeds which we plant; we gather seeds of other kinds and chart them, collecting, labeling and sometimes eating them:

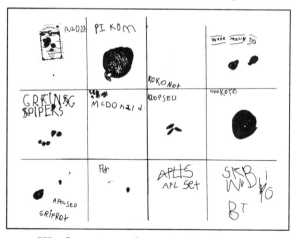

radish
pine cone
coconut
watermelon seeds

green peppers
McDonalds (from a Happy Meal)
cantaloupe seed
avocado

apple seed/grapefruit
pear
apple seed
?

We document the growth of our sunflowers and marigolds with daily log entries. Older children learn to read text, use an index and obtain information from pictures. They learn to write letters to primary resources, counting days on the calendar waiting for a reply. During a Japan study, Tara and Jennifer write this letter to a former Japanese student teacher requesting information about Japanese volcanoes:

Dear toshiko we are
In Mary class. are howl
Class IS STODiNG JapaN
me aND JeNNifer IS DOiNg
a saPraT ThiNg on VoLcaNos
AND we neeD SoMe aNDFrmashon
On MONTaN foDJgy WaLL you
PLes saNb us SoMe aNDFrMashon
to us
                  Love tara AND
R.S.   Mary   ToLD Jennifer K,
ThaT   us
foDJgy   you   Lavd   BY MTaN
            ThaT IS whay
we   rowT
Awakening   Seed   School

1130 W.   23rd   Street Tere nz 85282

Dear Toshi

We are in Mary's class. Our whole class is studying Japan. Me and Jennifer is doing a separate thing on volcanoes and we need some information on Mountain Fuji. Will you please send us some information to us?

Love, Tara and Jennifer K.

P.S. Mary told us that you lived by Mountain Fuji. That is why we wrote.

Awakening Seed School
1130 W. 23rd Street Tempe
AZ 85282

The children keep research notebooks. They take notes and draw pictures of the data collected. They may jot informational notes on scrap paper as they browse through the pictures in reference books, helping each other in the process. J.J. beams a smile of appreciation at Maureen when she discovers photographs of Japanese boats, his topic of research, in a *National Geographic* magazine. They learn to examine the nature of their topic, reflect on its meaning and interpret the information they've discovered as they read, write and talk to each other.

Expressing

As information is collected, plans begin to surface for demonstrating evidence of learning through the expressive arts. Written documents, art projects, dances, plays and oral reports are a few ways in which knowledge is expressed. Small groups of five-year-olds work cooperatively to produce a book of stories that synthesize information learned in their most recent study:

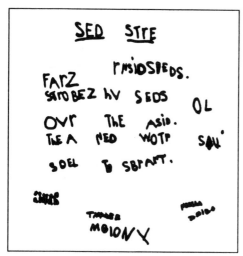

Seed Story

Flowers are in seeds. Strawberries have seeds all over the outside. They need water, sun and soil to sprout.

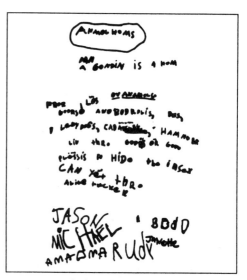

Flowers growing

Flowers make us feel good. They smell like candy. Pick flowers for your mom. They are the colors of the rainbow.

Seeds Growing

Seeds need soil and water. They won't grow without roots. Little plants are inside seeds. Seeds are large and small.

Animal Homes

A garden is a home for lots of animals. Gophers and butterflies, bees, ladybugs, caterpillars and hummingbirds live there. Gardens are good places to hide. The insects can eat there.

The same children duplicate the school rose garden with paper roses, covering one whole wall of the room, borrowing landscaping ideas from *The Rose in My Garden*. The garden needs insects, so we use new-found knowledge of insects and their habitats to fashion honey bees and ladybugs. *The Grouchy Ladybug* is consulted to find out what aphids look like so that they too can be cut from paper and added to the garden for ladybugs to consume.

In conjunction with written work (or in lieu of it), children may choose to create individual projects. Possibilities include dioramas, posters, paintings, clay figures, collages, paper sculptures, miniature figurines, wooden constructions, relief maps and food. Regardless of the nature of the project, the children need a plan. At this stage it's important to model how to plan and carry out work in an organized fashion.

We've found it helpful to give each child or team a cardboard box or container in which to store their materials. After a mini-lesson on how to write a project plan, they tape their plan to the side of their cardboard box so they can keep their materials organized as they become more independent:

During this phase children need long periods of time to develop their ideas and produce quality work. It may end up taking several whole days, or an hour or two a day over the course of many weeks, for them to process their knowledge and transform it into an expressed form. But it's during these work times that we discover the extent of their understanding as they converse with each other.

Celebrating

When learners have worked hard to unveil new information and express their knowledge in some chosen form, it's vital that they have an opportunity to share what they've learned. A range of possibilities exists for this important phase: celebration of knowledge can involve no more than simply hanging a piece of writing on the classroom wall.

One class paints "after Monet" tempera flowers using colors similar to those used by the artist in his water-lily series. A page in *Linea in Monet's Garden*, featuring a close-up of his brushstrokes on one particular water lily, provides further inspiration. The finished paintings, with titles and labels, are hung in the cafeteria as part of a school-wide study of different countries.

Projects can be shared in a variety of ways. One group chooses to perform a dance or play of a story that has had significance for them, or the entire class decides to organize a festival or open-house for parents and the entire school. Following the study of Japan, the children perform a dance based on *The Big Wave*, artfully display their projects, complete with a guidebook, and prepare mounds of authentic Japanese food for families and friends.

As the spring study nears its end, the children list what they've learned. A web of newly acquired data on gardens covers a large piece of mural paper. Information falls into three main groups: seeds, flowers and animal habitats. Using the webbed information, the children write three finished stories, bind them together and reproduce them for each member of the class. A dramatic performance of *The Carrot Seed*, with its message of patience, hope and new growth, happily celebrates the end of the story.

It's important to remember that the various phases are not separate, but interconnected and simultaneous. Rather than being linear and isolated one from the other, long-term content studies use eclectic sources and a large, accessible, stable body of literature, augmenting and connecting each other while building in an ever-spiraling fashion. Past studies are kept alive in the memories and the physical surroundings of the learning community and add to whatever content inquiries are current.

We've learned that no study is finite. Future studies, though perhaps chosen independently of previous ones, always build on what has gone before. Because an in-depth study is by definition multi-dimensional, content phases draw on the past, the present and even the future, at the same time drawing on each other. Spider lore from a Halloween symbol investigation, and *The Very Busy Spider* from an author study of Eric Carle, are remembered. Predator/prey knowledge first learned during a fall skeletal study surfaces when the class sees a hungry cat pursuing a mouse through his hiding place, the thick flowers of *The Rose in My Garden*.

Long after a study is formally over, children continue to bring in related books, information from newspapers and magazines, artifacts and specimens. Months after her class study of Japan is completed, Mia races into the classroom proudly sharing a piece of special Japanese paper her sister's birthday gift was wrapped in, exclaiming, "Look, it's Japanese!" The children keep making connections; they keep noticing things in a new way; they continue telling other people their discoveries and sharing their knowledge.

Content studies offer an opportunity for genuine learning. The interests of young children are awakened because they care about what they're studying and are naturally motivated. They teach themselves what they need to know — how to read for information, how to express their thoughts clearly in writing, and how to work with others to construct projects. Content studies further learners' knowledge of the world, while contributing to an understanding of the nature of learning with others. Individuals find that they've learned more, more pleasurably, because they've learned as a community.

Conclusion

Communities have been around for as long as there have been people. Throughout history we've learned together through work and play; we've pooled our thoughts to wonder at the meaning of worldly phenomena; we've depended on each other for survival. Oral traditions, sacred rites and the practices of daily living have all been passed from one generation to the next as part of community living.

During the early part of this century, great thinkers like John Dewey wondered how the idea of community related to an educational setting, and concluded that: *The school or classroom should be organized as a cooperative community so that the child can develop the attitudes and dispositions necessary for a responsible member of a democratic society* (George Dykhuizen, *The Life and Mind of John Dewey*, 1973). Dewey also maintained that we should use the children's own ideas and interests to make the curriculum more meaningful.

In looking back at the work we've done, we've discovered other "old-fashioned" ideas — for example, that good scholarship is essential, and that the best way to develop it is through practice. It naturally follows when an entire community takes learning seriously, living a life dedicated to the communal pursuit of knowledge. And when a group decides to make learning its life work, individuals flourish, knowing that their ideas are valued and appreciated by the other members of the community.

Those old ideas about the power of learning together lead us to the following beliefs:

- Children are knowledgeable. By listening to them we gain insight into how we can improve our craft as teachers.

- Real life phenomena can and should influence the work of the classroom community. Meaningful content and community work together to increase the learning power of both the individual and the group. Living an examined life, with time for understanding, allows the learner to know and remember.

- Diversity and inventiveness must be valued. Teachers and children need support for their efforts. Their pioneering work deserves to be celebrated at all levels by the entire community.

- Daily teaching and learning with children requires that we continually restructure how we work and think. The classroom and the curriculum need predictability, yet flexibility, to allow spontaneous learning to happen.

- We'll reach the individual if we care about the group. Conversely, the group will flourish if we care about the individual. By working to design a learning environment that is conducive to community, all learners will come to know their highest potential.

Community, always . . .

Some months ago, a silent stretch of asphalt through Monument Valley became our story road. Backdropped by some of the world's most awe-inspiring scenery, the stories first started emerging during our frequent travels between Kayenta and Mexican Hat, Utah. The extended period of time we spent in northern Arizona, working with teachers to make their schools a better place, provided an opportunity for us to see the universals in the stories we were exchanging. Eventually those stories began to blend together, and out of that blending a new story unfolded, the story of this book. But while the road through Monument Valley gave birth to the book, people in each of our lives played significant roles in bringing it to print.

Mary Anne Clark revealed the daily joy of literature, and Ken Bacher brought early inspiration for writing. Joan Moyer, Caryl Steere, Merri Schall, Carole Edelsky, Virginia Opincar and Pam Miles influenced our thinking early on in our training as teachers. Carole Christine's tireless work with s.m.i.l.e. (Support Maintenance and Implementation of Language Expression) and C.E.D. (Center for Establishing Dialogue in Teaching and Learning) gave us a community of forward-thinking educators to exchange ideas with and grow with as professionals, knowing that we weren't alone. Through this grass-roots network of colleagues we became empowered as thinkers and teachers because of our affiliations with others.

Over the years we've been inspired by the work and thinking of Karen Smith and Pam Clark, who never seem to view an obstacle as insurmountable. Our views of teaching and learning have been greatly influenced by Chris Boyd and Yvonne Mersereau as well, two of the finest practitioners around. Their work with content, literature and dialogue has served as a catalyst for our thinking about curriculum design. They consistently remind us to keep our standards high.

We're grateful to Mary Ellen Giacobbe for so clearly demonstrating the link between literature and writing. Personally witnessing her honest way of listening to children has helped both of us to become better at our craft as teachers. At the same time, Don Murray taught us to sit down and write, to get beyond the critic within ourselves that kept us from making writing a regular part of our lives as teachers. Through example, he showed us that to be a teacher of writing you have to be a writer, and that writing should be a natural outgrowth of our profession as teachers. Maryann Eeds and Elaine Surbeck also provided endless support. They both believed in our work all along and helped us to view ourselves as competent practitioners by encouraging us to commit our ideas to print. We're especially appreciative of their input to our earlier manuscripts.

During the year we wrote the book we were fortunate to work alongside Becky Lewis and Janice Woodhull in our classrooms. They each gave us the gift of a year of dialogue, feedback and daily reflection on the details, great and small, in our classroom communities. Their hard work and attention to detail made an invaluable contribution to this book. We were also influenced significantly by the staffs at Kayenta Boarding School and Aneth Community School. The days we spent with these fine people provided powerful fuel for the ideas that came forth. More than anything, they listened to us and reminded us our stories were worth telling.

Our work simply couldn't have happened without the constant support of a few noteworthy individuals: Jaimie, May, Erma, Annie and Al all gave energy to the project by believing in us and always being there when we needed them; the staff at Awakening Seed School contributed to our work through daily efforts to keep the dream of better schooling alive; Bill and John and our children allowed us a full year of Wednesday nights at the computer so the book could be written.

The children in our classrooms were, of course, the compelling reason for writing. We're indebted to them for being our teachers as we struggled to put new thought into practice. We're also grateful to Adrian Peetoom, our editor, for bringing clarity to our work, and for having the vision to see our classroom stories in print.

And finally we wish to acknowledge our friend and mentor, Ralph Peterson, who played a major role in our transformation as educational thinkers. It was from Ralph that we first began to understand the power of community. Through his example we were able to approach our teaching and our lives as a continuous process of vision and revision. He modeled the kind of teaching with adults that he expected us to use with children, and through this we learned to be reflective in our practice as teachers. Our developing commitment to literacy was an ongoing gift from Ralph: he encouraged us to pursue new ideas and eagerly helped us process what we saw happening in our classrooms; he believed in us and enabled us to believe in ourselves.

References

Aardema, Verna. *Bringing the Rain to Kapiti Plain.*

Ahlberg, Janet and Allan. *The Jolly Postman.*

Base, Graeme. *Animalia.*

Buck, Pearl S. *The Big Wave.*

Carle, Eric. *The Very Busy Spider.*

Carle, Eric. *The Grouchy Ladybug.*

Cole, Joanna. *Bony-Legs.*

Day, Alexandra. *Good Dog, Carl.*

De Paola, Tomie. *Nana Upstairs and Nana Downstairs.*

Fox, Mem. *Wilfrid Gordon McDonald Partridge.*

Gerstein, Mordecai. *Mountains of Tibet.*

Hall, Donald. *The Ox-Cart Man.*

Heyward, Du Bose. *The Country Bunny and The Little Gold Shoes.*

Hazen, Barbara. *Tight Times.*

Hurd, Thacher. *Mystery on the Docks.*

Johnson, Tony. *Yonder.*

Khalsa, Dayal K. *Tales of a Gambling Grandma.*

Krauss, Ruth. *The Carrot Seed.*

Lobel, Arnold. *Frog and Toad.*

Lobel, Arnold. *Frog and Toad Are Friends.*

Lobel, Arnold. *The Rose in My Garden.*

McDermott, Gerald. *The Magic Tree.*

Musgrove, Margaret W. *Ashanti to Zulu.*

Sendak, Maurice. *Chicken Soup with Rice.*

Sendak, Maurice. *Outside Over There.*

Steig, William. *The Amazing Bone.*

Steig, William. *Amos and Boris.*

Traditional. *Peach Boy* (Japan).

Traditional. *The Snow Child* (Russia).

Tresselt, Alvin. *The Mitten.*

Van Allsburg, Chris. *Ben's Dream.*

Van Allsburg, Chris. *Jumanji.*

Van Allsburg, Chris. *Polar Express.*

Van Allsburg, Chris. *The Stranger.*

Waber, Bernard. *Rich Cat, Poor Cat.*

White, E.B. *Charlotte's Web.*

Williams, Vera. *A Chair for My Mother.*

Yolen, Jane. *Three Bears Rhyme Book.*